The Wood is Sweet

JOHN CLARE

THE WOOD IS SWEET

Poems of Clare selected and introduced

by

David Powell

Illustrated by Carry Akroyd

THE JOHN CLARE SOCIETY

John Clare

born 13 July 1793 at Helpston

died 20 May 1864 at the Northampton Asylum

The Wood is Sweet, 2005

ISBN 0-9538995-5-1

©2005 Introduction & selection David Powell

©2005 Illustrations Carry Akroyd

The John Clare Society
Helpston, Peterborough
www.johnclare.org.uk

Printed by Lightning Source

Set in Calisto MT

FOREWORD

The Wood is Sweet was first published by The Bodley Head in 1966 and reprinted in 1971, with illustrations by John O'Connor. During recent years the John Clare Society has increasingly felt the need for a modest and attractive book to introduce new readers to a manageable selection of Clare's huge output. We therefore asked David Powell if he would revisit his early selection and prepare it for a new edition. He has added a few poems, re-ordered some, slightly revised the text and punctuation as he thought desirable, and written a new introduction which incorporates extracts from Clare's autobiographical writings.

For very many years David Powell has worked with Eric Robinson and others to produce the great Oxford edition of Clare's poems, and on the Carcanet prose volume, *John Clare by Himself. The Wood is Sweet* draws on his great editorial experience and knowledge of the poet.

For this edition the John Clare Society has commissioned Carry Akroyd to provide illustrations. She is an artist who has established a reputation for her images of wildlife and the countryside, and she has a deep understanding of Clare's poetry; it has inspired her work for a number of years. Carry Akroyd lives in Northamptonshire near the scenes which Clare himself loved and described.

Peter Cox
for the John Clare Society

I would not that my being all should die
  And pass away with every common lot,
I would not that my humble dust should lie
  In quite a strange and unfrequented spot
  By all unheeded and by all forgot,
With nothing save the heedless winds to sigh
And nothing but the dewy morn to weep
  About my grave far hid from the world's eye.
I feign would have some friend to wander nigh
  And find a path to where my ashes sleep;
Not the cold heart that merely passes by
  To read who lieth there, but such that keep
Past memories warm with deeds of other years
And pay to friendship some few friendly tears.

John Clare's "Memory"

CONTENTS

INTRODUCTION

John Clare is accepted today as one of the great English poets, along with his contemporaries Wordsworth, Coleridge, Byron, Keats, Shelley and Blake. It was not always so.

There was an early false dawn when Clare's first volume of poems, *Poems Descriptive of Rural Life and Scenery,* was published in 1820. It sold some 3,000 copies in the first year, outselling Wordsworth and Keats. Clare enjoyed a brief fame and visited London four times. He was marketed as 'the peasant poet', but this was at a time when the fashion for peasant poetry was beginning to decline. 'Peasant poet' meant ill-educated and poor, and hinted that it was remarkable that Clare could write poetry at all, let alone great poetry.

His later volumes sold progressively less well, though the poetry itself steadily improved. He spent the last 27 years of his life in mental institutions, largely forgotten by the public outside. He continued to write poetry. In all he wrote more than 3,000 poems or fragments, perhaps the largest output of any of the great English poets.

Small selections from his work were published in 1873, 1901, 1908, and then a revival began with editions by Edmund Blunden (who introduced the first edition of this book) in 1920 and 1924. The large two-volume J.W. Tibble edition appeared in 1935, and in 1949 Geoffrey Grigson gave us *Poems of John Clare's Madness*. These works contained numerous inaccuracies. Clare remained a 'minor' poet in universities and literary histories.

1

In 1964 the centenary of Clare's death was commemorated, and work started on the complete Oxford English Texts edition. This was completed in nine volumes 39 years later in 2003 and so narrowly escaped J.C. Squire's condemnation of 1921 that "an edition of him in ten volumes would be a monument not to his genius but to an admirer's folly". Jonathan Bate's important biography appeared later in 2003. Between 1964 and 2004 there has been a range of selections, research papers, articles and theses, far more than in the whole of the period before 1964.

The first edition of *The Wood is Sweet* was published in 1966. On its dust jacket we were told that

> to read Clare is to look through a microscope at nature, to see and breathe the countryside. It is the pastoral scene he describes, a countryside of shepherds, ploughmen and milkmaids, of peace and birdsong – a scene that is today fast disappearing, or has already gone, and is therefore the more nostalgic.

In 1981 the John Clare Society was formed, and the first issue of the Journal leads off:

> John Clare was not an ordinary man and certainly not an ordinary poet. He came very close to greatness and, but for an accident of birth, might have been more readily thought of as a great poet. Equally, but for that accident of birth in a peasant's cottage in Helpston, we might not have heard of him at all.

> Fortunately his reputation today extends far beyond that parish boundary and with the help of the society we can all work towards establishing the true recognition which he deserves in the world of

literature. There has been no other poet like him, nor can there be again.

It is fitting therefore that the John Clare Society should publish the second edition of *The Wood is Sweet.*

The presentation of the poems needs a brief comment. I have largely followed Kelsey Thornton's method in his short Everyman edition of Clare in 1997. The Oxford English Texts edition follows the manuscripts and prints the poems exactly as Clare wrote them, leaving it to others to decide and argue what he ought to have written. However, I realise that the newcomer to Clare may be put off by the resulting strangeness, and have therefore added a strictly limited amount of punctuation including apostrophes, normalised Clare's spelling (e.g. 'than' not 'then', 'pigeon' not 'piegon'), and ignored his ampersand. Dialect words are retained, and the reader should refer to the Glossary at the end of the book.

Clare's life and poetry are inseparable and his determination to succeed knew no bounds. The autobiographical paragraphs which follow will, I hope, help the reader to understand Clare better.

David Powell
February 2005

never a leisure hour passed me without making use of it   every winter night our once unlettered hut was wonderfully changed in its appearance to a school room   the old table, which old as it was doubtless never was honoured with higher employment all its days than the convenience of bearing at meal times the luxury of a barley loaf or dish of potatoes, was now covered with the rude beginnings of scientifical requisitions, pens, ink, and paper one hour, jobbling the pen at sheep hooks and tarbottles, and another trying on a slate a knotty question in numeration, or pounds, shillings and pence...

There is nothing but poetry about the existence of childhood real simple soul-moving poetry the laughter and joy of poetry and not its philosophy and there is nothing of poetry about manhood but the reflection and the remembrance of what has been   nothing more

I loved to employ leisure when a boy in wandering about the fields watching the habits of birds to see the woodpecker sweeing away in its ups and downs and the jay bird chattering by the wood side its restless warnings of passing clowns   the travels of insects where the black beetle nimbled along and the opening of field flowers   such amusements gave me the greatest of pleasures but I could not account for the reason why they did so

I thought I was up sooner than usual and before morning was on the stir out of doors but I am pleasantly disappointed by the whistle of the ploughboy past the window making himself merry and trying to make the dull weather dance to a very pleasant tune which I know well and yet cannot recollect the song but there are hundreds of these pleasant tunes familiar to the plough and splashing team and the little fields of spring that have lain out the brown rest of winter and green into mirth with the sprouting grain the songs of the skylark and the

4

old songs and ballads that ever accompany field happiness in following the plough — but neither heard known or noticed by all the world beside

Among all the friendships I have made in life those of school friendship and childish acquaintance are the sweetest to remember   there is no deception among them there is nothing of regret in them but the loss   they are the fairest and sunniest pages memory ever doubles down in the checkered volume of life to refer to   there is no blotches upon them — they are not found like bargains on matters of interest nor broken for selfish ends — I made but few close friendships for I found few with the like tastes inclinations and feelings

My acquaintance of books is not so good as later opportunities might have made it for I cannot and never could plod through every a book in a regular mechanical way   as I meet with it I dip into it here and there and if it does not suit I lay it down and seldom take it up again

To look at nature with a poetic feeling magnifies the pleasure yet naturalists and botanists seem to have little or no taste for this sort of feeling they merely make a collection of dried specimens classing them after Linnaeus into tribes and families as a sort of curiosity and fame   I have nothing of this curiosity about me though I feel as happy as they can in finding a new species of field flower or butterfly which I have not before seen   yet I have no desire further to dry the plant or torture the butterfly by sticking it on a cork board with a pin I have no wish to do this if my feelings would let me

I only wish them to settle on a flower till I can come up with them to examine the powdered colours on their wings and then they may flutter off from fancied danger and welcome   I feel gratified

I never had much relish for the pastimes of youth   instead of going out on the green at the town end on winter Sundays to play football I stuck to my corner stool poring over a book   in fact I grew so fond of being alone at last that my mother was fain to force me into company for the neighbours had assured her mind into the fact that I was no better than crazy   at length my schooldays was to be at an end as I was thought learned enough for my intended trade which was to be a shoemaker

As I grew up a man I mixed more in company and frequented dancings for the sake of meeting with the lasses for I was a lover very early in life my first attachment being a schoolboy affection but Mary — who cost me more ballads than sighs was beloved with a romantic or platonic sort of feeling
if I could but gaze on her face or fancy a smile on her countenance it was sufficient... she was a beautiful girl and as the dream never awoke into reality her beauty was always fresh in my memory she is still unmarried

I always wrote my poems in great haste and generally finished them at once whether long or short for if I did not they generally were left unfinished   what corrections I made I always made them while writing the poem and never could do anything with them afterwards

A religion that teaches us to act justly to speak truth and love mercy ought to be held sacred in every country and whatever the differences of creeds may be in lighter matters they ought to be overlooked and the principle respected

although I never saw a book on grammar before I was 20 or knew anything whatever of the proper construction of sentences — yet I was so far benefited from reading an old newspaper now and then as to write pretty correctly and never any otherwise than to be intelligible although before this I could not scarcely write a common letter so as to understand it myself

Found several pieces of Roman pot in Harrison's top close on the hill over which the road crosses to the Tindhills at the north east corner of Oxey wood   one piece was the letter V   Artis says they are Roman and I verily believe some Roman camp or pottery was made there

MONTH BY MONTH

FLOWERS

Ere yet the year is one month old
    In spite of frost and wind and snow
Bare bosomed to the quaking cold
    Spring's little self-sown flowers will blow,
And ever kin to early hours
    Peep aconites in cups of gold
With frilled leaves muffled round their flowers
    Like tender maidens shunning cold;

And then as winter's parting pledge
    Like true love in his crabbed reign
The violet 'neath the naked hedge
    Peeps through the rustling leaves again,
Soon as from off the thicket's moss
    The sunshine clears the doubting snow
And the o'erjoyed and neighing horse
    Can find a patch of green to blow.

Like jewels brought by early hours
    These little littered blossoms come,
Like wanderers from fairy bowers
    They smile and gladly find a home;
And on the threshold of the spring
    Like timid childern out of doors
They lie and wait the birds to sing
    And laugh upon the splashy moors,

Till April's smiling frowning weather
    Like younkers to a holiday
The comers troop in crowds together
    To wait the feast of merry May,
In sunny nooks and shelter nursed
    Buds all their early blooms display
Where sunbeams show their faces first
    And make when there the longest stay.

FIRST SIGHT OF SPRING

The hazel blooms in threads of crimson hue
    Peep through the swelling buds and look for spring
Ere yet a whitethorn leaf appears in view
    Or March finds throstles pleased enough to sing;
    On the old touchwood tree woodpeckers cling
A moment, and their harsh-toned notes renew,
    In happier mood the stock-dove claps his wing,
The squirrel sputters up the powdered oak
    With tail cocked o'er his head and ears erect
Startled to hear the woodman's understroke,
    And with the courage which his fears collect
He hisses fierce half malice and half glee,
Leaping from branch to branch about the tree,
    In winter's foliage, moss and lichens, dressed.

SPRING

What charms does nature at the spring put on
    When hedges unperceived get stained in green,
When even moss that gathers on the stone
    Crowned with its little knobs of flowers is seen,
And every road and lane through field and glen
    Triumphant boasts a garden of its own.
In spite of trampling horse with cart and plough
And nipping sheep and tented hungry cow,
    The little daisy finds a place to blow,
And where old winter leaves her splashy slough
    The lady-smocks will not disdain to grow,
And dandelions like to suns will bloom
    Aside some bank or hillock creeping low,
Though each too often meet an hasty doom
    From trampling clowns who heed not where they go.

HOME PICTURES IN MAY

The sunshine bathes in clouds of many hues
And morning's feet are gemmed with early dews,
Warm daffodils about the garden beds
Peep through their pale slim leaves their golden heads,
Sweet earthly suns of spring — the gosling broods,
In coats of sunny green, about the road
Waddle in ecstasy — and in rich moods
The old hen leads her flickering chicks abroad,
Oft scuttling 'neath her wings to see the kite
Hang wavering o'er them in the spring's blue light.
The sparrows round their new nests chirp with glee
And sweet the robin spring's young luxury shares,
Tootling its song in feathery gooseberry tree
While watching worms the gardener's spade unbares.

JUNE

Now summer is in flower and nature's hum
Is never silent round her sultry bloom,
Insects as small as dust have never done
Wi' glittering dance and reeling in the sun,
And green wood fly and blossom haunting bee
Are never weary of their melody.
Round field hedge now flowers in full glory twine,
Large bindweed bells, wild hop, and streaked woodbine
That lift athirst their slender-throated flowers,
Agape for dew-falls and for honey showers;
These round each bush in sweet disorder run
And spread their wild hues to the sultry sun,
Where its silk netting lace on twigs and leaves
The mottled spider at eve's leisure weaves,
That every morning meet the poet's eye
Like fairies' dew-wet dresses hung to dry...

from *The Shepherd's Calendar*

SUMMER MOODS

I love at eventide to walk alone
   Down narrow lanes o'erhung with dewy thorn
Where from the long grass underneath — the snail
   Jet-black creeps out and sprouts his timid horn.
I love to muse o'er meadows newly mown
   Where withering grass perfumes the sultry air,
Where bees search round with sad and weary drone
   In vain for flowers that bloomed but newly there;
While in the juicy corn the hidden quail
   Cries 'wet my foot' and hid as thoughts unborn
The fairylike and seldom-seen landrail
   Utters 'craik craik' like voices underground,
Right glad to meet the evening's dewy veil
   And see the light fade into glooms around.

SUMMER IMAGES

AN EXTRACT

I love at early morn from new-mown swath
 To see the startled frog his route pursue,
And mark while leaping o'er the dripping path
 His bright sides scatter dew,
And early lark that from its bustle flies —
 To hail his matin new,
   And watch him to the skies;

And note on hedgerow baulks in moisture sprent
 The jetty snail creep from the mossy thorn
In earnest heed and tremulous intent,
 Frail brother of the morn,
That from the tiny bents and misted leaves
 Withdraws his timid horn,
   And fearful vision weaves;

And swallows heed on smoke tanned chimney top
 As wont be first unsealing morning's eye,
Ere yet the bee hath gleaned one wayward drop
 Of honey on his thigh,
And see him seek morn's airy couch to sing
 Until the golden sky
   Besprents his russet wing;

And sawning boy by tanning corn espy
 With clapping noise to startle birds away,
And hear him brawl to every passer-by
 To know the hour of day,
And see the uncradled breeze refreshed and strong
 With waking blossoms play,
   And breathe Aeolian song.

16

I love the south-west wind, or low or loud,
    And not the less when sudden drops of rain
Moisten my pallid cheek from ebon cloud
    Threatening soft showers again,
That over lands new ploughed and meadow grounds
    Summer's sweet breath unchains
        And wakes harmonious sounds.

Rich music breathes in summer's every sound
    And in her harmony of varied greens,
Woods, meadows, hedgerows, cornfields, all around
    Much beauty intervenes,
Filling with harmony the ear and eye,
    While o'er the mingling scenes
        Far spreads the laughing sky.

And wind-enamoured aspen — mark the leaves
    Turn up their silver lining to the sun,
And list the brustling noise that oft deceives,
    And makes the sheep boy run;
The sound so mimics fast approaching showers
    He thinks the rain begun,
        And hastes to sheltering bowers…

THE WOODLAND STILE

When one's been walking in the open plain
   Where the sun ne'er winks his eye, 'tis sweet awhile
To meet the shadows of a narrow lane
   Or quiet arbour of a woodland stile,
To sit and hear the little bees complain
   Among the woodbine blossoms o'er their toil,
And the hoarse murmurs of the distant swain
   Driving his horses o'er the sunburnt soil;
While shadows hide me and leaves entertain
   My fancies with their freaks around my seat,
Dancing and whispering with the wooing wind
   Like lovers o'er their secrets — while the heat
Glimmers without and can no passage find
   To hurt the joys which rest so longed to meet.

FIELD THOUGHTS

Field thoughts to me are happiness and joy,
    When I can lie upon the pleasant grass
Or track some little path and so employ
    My mind in trifles, pausing as I pass
The little wild-flower clumps by nothing nursed
    But dews and sunshine and impartial rain,
And welcomely to quench my summer thirst
    I bend me by the flaggy dyke to gain
Dewberries so delicious to the taste;
    And then I wind the flag-fringed meadow lake
And mark the pike plunge with unusual haste
    Through water-weeds and many a circle make,
While bursts of happiness from heaven fall;
There all have hopes; here fields are free for all.

FIR WOOD

The firs that taper into twigs and wear
The rich blue green of summer all the year,
Softening the roughest tempest almost calm,
And offering shelter ever still and warm
To the small path that travels underneath,
Where loudest winds almost as summer's breath
 Scarce fan the weed that lingers green below,
When others out of doors are lost in frost and snow,
And sweet the music trembles on the ear
As the wind suthers through each tiny spear,
Makeshifts for leaves, and yet so rich they show
Winter is almost summer where they grow.

THE AUTUMN ROBIN

AN EXTRACT

Sweet little bird in russet coat,
    The livery of the closing year,
I love thy lonely plaintive note
    And tiny whispering song to hear.
While on the stile or garden seat
    I sit to watch the falling leaves,
The song thy little joys repeat
    My loneliness relieves…

AUTUMN

I love the fitful gust that shakes
   The casement all the day,
And from the mossy elm tree takes
   The faded leaf away,
Twirling it by the window pane
With thousand others down the lane.

I love to see the shaking twig
   Dance till the shut of eve,
The sparrow on the cottage rig,
   Whose chirp would make believe
That spring was just now flirting by
In summer's lap with flowers to lie.

I love to see the cottage smoke
   Curl upwards through the naked trees,
The pigeons nestled round the cote
   On dull November days like these,
The cock upon the dunghill crowing,
The mill sails on the heath a-going.

The feather from the raven's breast
   Falls on the stubble lea,
The acorns near the old crow's nest
   Fall pattering down the tree,
The grunting pigs that wait for all
Scramble and hurry where they fall.

NOVEMBER

The shepherds almost wonder where they dwell,
    And the old dog for his right journey stares,
The path leads somewhere but they cannot tell,
    And neighbour meets with neighbour unawares.
The maiden passes close beside her cow
    And wonders on and thinks her far away;
The ploughman goes unseen behind his plough
    And seems to lose his horses half the day.
The lazy mist creeps on in journey slow,
The maidens shout and wonder where they go,
    So dull and dark are the November days.
The lazy mist high up the evening curled,
    And now the morn quite hides in smoky haze,
The place we occupy seems all the world.

THE LAST OF AUTUMN

AN EXTRACT

Come bleak November in thy wildness come,
    Thy mornings clothed in rime, thy evenings chill;
E'en they have powers to tempt me from my home,
    E'en they have beauties to delight me still.
Though nature lingers in her mourning weeds
    And wails the dying year in gusty blast,
Still added beauty to her end proceeds
    And wildness triumphs when her bloom is past.

Though long grass all the day is drenched in dew
    And splashy pathways lead one o'er the greens,
Though naked fields hang lonely on the view,
    Long lost to harvest and its busy scenes,
Yet in the distance shines the painted bough,
    Leaves changed to every colour ere they die,
And through the valleys rivers whiten now,
    Once little brooks which summer dribbled dry...

SNOWSTORM (1)

What a night. The wind howls, hisses, and but stops
    To howl more loud, while the snow volley keeps
        Incessant batter at the window pane,
        Making our comfort feel as sweet again;
And in the morning when the tempest drops,
    At every cottage door mountainous heaps
Of snow lies drifted that all entrance stops
        Until the besom and the shovel gains
The path — and leaves a wall on either side —
The shepherd, rambling valleys white and wide,
    With new sensations his old memories fills,
When hedges left at night, no more descried,
    Are turned to one white sweep of curving hills,
And trees turned bushes half their bodies hide.

SNOWSTORM (2)

Winter is come in earnest, and the snow
    In dazzling splendour — crumping underfoot
Spreads a white world all calm, and where we go
    By hedge or wood trees shine from top to root
In feathered foliage, flashing light and shade
    Of strangest contrast — fancy's pliant eye
Delighted sees a vast romance displayed,
    And fairy halls descended from the sky;
The smallest twig its snowy burthen wears,
    And woods o'erhead the dullest eyes engage
To shape strange things — where arch and pillar bears
    A roof of grains fantastic arched and high,
And little shed beside the spinney wears
    The grotesque semblance of an hermitage.

CHRISTMAS

Christmas is come, and every hearth
Makes room to give him welcome now.
E'en want will dry its tears in mirth
And crown him wi' a holly bough,
Though tramping 'neath a winter sky
O'er snow track paths and rimy stiles;
The huswife sets her spinning by
And bids him welcome wi' her smiles.

Each house is swept the day before
And windows stuck wi' evergreens,
The snow is besomed from the door
And comfort crowns the cottage scenes,
Gilt holly wi' its thorny pricks
And yew and box wi' berries small,
These deck the unused candlesticks
And pictures hanging by the wall.

Neighbours resume their annual cheer,
Wishing wi' smiles and spirits high
Glad Christmas and a happy year
To every morning passer-by,
Milk maids their Christmas journeys go
Accompanied wi' favoured swain,
And childern pace the crumping snow
To taste their granny's cake again.

from *The Shepherd's Calendar*

NATURE

There is a charm in nature felt and seen
In every season of the varied year,
In winter's frost, in spring's reviving green,
   'Tis everywhere.

In foreign lands how beautiful the sight
Over a thousand mountains of snow spray
With nought of green — but mountains pale as light
   And all the way.

The spring's green herbage full of flowers
And fields where lives the lark mid greener grain,
We love and worship them in April hours,
   Then wish again

That spring with all her joys would longer last;
But summer with young buds is left to choose
And brings once more in memory of the past
   Flowers of all hues.

Then autumn red and yellow quickly pass
Like broods of nestling birds upon the wing,
Till all is gone and nothing but the grass
   Remembers spring.

The wind, the shower, the drapery of the sky
When day cools over meadows into dun,
And clouds in gold and crimson glories lie
   In set of sun,

A globe of fire and as a table round,
Then wastes to half, still shutting out the day,
Till the curved rim drops quickly in the ground,
   And all is grey.

HOUR BY HOUR

BREAK OF DAY

The lark he rises early,
    And the ploughman goes away
Before it's morning fairly
    At the guessing break of day;
The fields lie in the dawning
    And the valley's hid in gold,
At the pleasant time of morning
    When the shepherd goes to fold.

The maiden laughs and hollos
    When she sees the feeding cows;
They switch their tails and follow
    Where she can't get over sloughs;
I love the gentle dawning
    And the valleys hid in gold,
At the pleasant time of morning
    When the shepherd goes to fold.

MORNING

The morning comes — the drops of dew
Hang on the grass and bushes too,
The sheep more eager bite the grass
Whose moisture gleams like drops of glass,
The heifer licks in grass and dew
That makes her drink and fodder too.
The little bird his morn song gives,
His breast wet with the dripping leaves,
Then stops abruptly just to fly
And catch the wakened butterfly
That goes to sleep behind the flowers
Or backs of leaves from dews and showers.
The yellowhammer haply blest
Sits by the dyke upon her nest,
The long grass hides her from the day,
The water keeps the boys away.
The morning sun is round and red
As crimson curtains round a bed,
The dew drops hang on barley horns
As beads the necklace thread adorns,
The dew drops hang wheat ears upon
Like golden drops against the sun,
Hedge sparrows in the bush cry 'tweet',
O'er nests larks winnow in the wheat,
Till the sun turns gold and gets more high,
And paths are clean and grass gets dry,
And longest shadows pass away,
And brightness is the blaze of day.

THE SCHOOLBOYS IN THE MORNING

The schoolboys in the morning soon as dressed
Went round the fields to play and look for nests.
They found a crow's but dare not climb so high,
And looked for nests when any bird was nigh;
At length they got agen a bush to play,
And found a pink's nest round and mossed with grey,
And lined about with feathers and with hair;
They tried to climb but brambles said 'forbear';
One found a stone and stronger than the rest,
And took another up to reach the nest,
'Here's eggs' they hollo'd with a hearty shout,
Small round and blotched, they reached and tore them out.
The old birds sat and hollo'd 'pink pink pink',
And cattle hurried to the pond to drink.

They stood to blow the eggs and rest awhile,
And the maid stood to scold them at the stile,
She stood and throwed her apron o'er her head
To shun the shower, but they heard nought she said,
Till the old bull came to the pond to cool,
And bellowed out and frit them all to school;
They ran away and tumbled o'er the hedge,
And tore their legs and waded through the sedge,
The old bull stared and bellowed with surprise,
And lashed the pond and shook away the flies.
They hurried on and scarcely dare to play,
And left the bull and bushes far away,
And when the pathway showed the town in sight
They hid the rest in rushes till the night.

NOON

The midday hour of twelve the clock counts o'er,
    A sultry stillness lulls the air asleep,
The very buzz of fly is heard no more,
    Nor one faint wrinkle o'er the waters creep.
Like one large sheet of glass the pool does shine
    Reflecting in its face the burnt sunbeam,
The very fish their sturting play decline
    Seeking the willow shadows 'side the stream,
And, where the hawthorn branches o'er the pool,
    The little bird forsaking song and nest
Flutters on dripping twigs his limbs to cool,
    And splashes in the stream his burning breast.
O free from thunder, for a sudden shower,
To cherish nature in this noonday hour.

THE WATER LILIES

The water lilies, white and yellow flowers,
    How beautiful they are upon the lake,
I've stood and looked upon the place for hours,
    And thought how fine a garden they would make.
The pleasant leaves upon the water float,
    The dragonfly would come and stay for hours,
And when the water pushed the pleasure boat,
    Would find a safer place among the flowers.
They lay like pleasure in a quiet place,
    Close where the moorhen loved her nest to make,
They lay like beauty with a smiling face,
    And I have called them 'ladies of the lake';
I've brought the longest pole and stood for hours,
And tried for years before I got those flowers.

FIELD FLOWERS

Hark from amid the corn that happy brawl —
    'Tis village childern running after flowers;
To this void bosom how the sounds recall
    Memories again of childhood's merry hours
When through the garden pales or o'er the wall
    We reach'd at garden flowers with eager hands,
Or boldly sought the field flowers free for all
    Wading breast high amid the green corn lands
For crimson poppies and corn bottles blue,
    Startling the partridge covey unawares
That o'er our head in wild disorder flew;
    Here we like them was blest, life laid no snares
To rob our joys, he was a partner too,
  Why did he turn a foe and fill our path with cares?

THE DOWNPOUR

The maiden ran away to fetch the clothes,
And threw her apron o'er her cap and bows,
But the shower caught her ere she hurried in,
And beat and almost dowsed her to the skin;
The ruts ran brooks as they would ne'er be dry,
And the boy waded as he hurried by,
The half drowned ploughman waded to the knees,
And birds were almost drowned upon the trees,
The streets ran rivers till they floated o'er,
And women screamed to meet it at the door;
Labour fled home and rivers hurried by,
   And still it fell as it would never stop,
E'en the old stone pit deep as house is high
   Was brimming o'er and floated o'er the top.

SUDDEN SHOWER

Black grows the southern sky betokening rain,
    And humming hive-bees homeward hurry by,
They feel the change — so let us shun the grain,
    And take the broad road while our feet are dry.
Ay, there some dropples moistened in my face,
    And pattered on my hat — 'tis coming nigh,
Let's look about, and find a sheltering place.
    The little things around like you and I
Are hurrying through the grass to shun the shower.
    Here stoops an ash tree – hark the wind gets high
But never mind; this ivy for an hour,
    Rain as it may, will keep us dryly here,
That little wren knows well his sheltering bower,
    Nor leaves his dry house though we come so near.

EVENING SCHOOLBOYS

Harken that happy shout — the school-house door
    Is open thrown and out the younkers teem,
Some run to leap-frog on the rushy moor,
    And others dabble in the shallow stream,
Catching young fish and turning pebbles o'er
    For mussel clams — Look in that yellow gleam
Where the retiring sun that rests the while
    Streams through the broken hedge — How happy seem
Those schoolboy friendships leaning o'er the stile,
    Both reading in one book — anon a dream,
Rich with new joys, doth their young hearts beguile,
    And the book's pocketed most hastily.
Ah, happy boys, well may ye turn and smile,
    When joys are yours that never cost a sigh.

CROWS CROWD QUAKING

Crows crowd quaking over head
Hastening to the woods to bed,
Cooing sits the lonely dove
Calling home her absent love,
Kirchup Kirchup 'mong the wheat,
Partridge distant partridge greet...

Bats flit by in hood and cowl,
Through the barn hole pops the owl,
From the hedge the beetles boom,
Heedless buzz and drowsy hum,
Haunting every bushy place,
Flopping in the labourer's face...

from *Summer Evening*

RECOLLECTIONS
AFTER AN EVENING WALK

Just as the even bell rung we set out
To wander the fields and the meadows about,
And the first thing we marked that was lovely to view
Was the sun hung on nothing and bidding adieu,
He seemed like a ball of pure gold in the west
In a cloud like a mountain blue dropping to rest;
The clouds all around him were tinged wi' his rays,
And trees at a distance seemed all on a blaze,
Till lower and lower and sunk from our sight,
And blue mist came creeping wi' silence and night.
The woodman then ceased wi' his hatchet to hack,
And bent away home wi' his kid on his back,
The mower too lapped up his scythe from our sight,
And put on his jacket and bid us good night,
The thresher once lumping we heard him no more,
He left his barn dust and had shut up his door,
The shepherd had told all his sheep in his pen,
And hummed his song to his cottage agen:
But the sweetest of all seeming music to me
Was the song of the clumsy brown beetle and bee,
The one was a-hastening away to his hive,
The other was just from his sleeping alive,
And our hats he kept knocking as if he'd no eyes,
And when battered down he was puzzled to rise.
The little gay moth too was lovely to view
A-dancing wi's lily-white wings in the dew,
He whisked o'er the water-pudge flirting and airy,
And perched on the down-headed grass like a fairy.
And there came the snail from his shell peeping out
As fearful and cautious as thieves on the rout,
The sly jumping frog too had ventured to tramp,
And the glow-worm had just 'gun to light up his lamp,
To sip of the dew the worm peeped from his den,

But dreading our footsteps soon vanished agen:
And numbers of creatures appeared in our sight
That live in the silence and sweetness of night,
Climbing up the tall grasses or scaling the bough,
But these were all nameless unnoticed till now.
And then we wound round 'neath the brook's willow row,
And looked at the clouds that kept passing below,
The moon's image too in the brook we could see't
As if 'twas the other world under our feet,
And we listened well pleased at the guggles and groans
The water made passing the pebbles and stones.
And then we turned up by the rut rifted lane,
And sought for our cot and the village again,
For night gathered round and shut all from the eye,
And a black sooty cloud crept all over the sky,
The wet bush we passed soon as touched it would drop,
And the grass 'neath our feet was as wet as a mop,
And as to the town we approached very fast,
The bat even popped in our face as he passed,
And the crickets sung loud as we went by the house,
And by the barn side we saw many a mouse
Quirking round for the kernels that littered about,
As shook from the straw which the thresher hurled out.
And then we came up to our cottage once more,
And shut out the night dew and locked up the door,
The dog barked a welcome well pleased at our sight,
And the owl o'er our cot flew and whooped a good night.

CLIFFORD HILL

The river rambles like a snake
    Along the meadow green,
And loud the noise the mill wheels make
    I' summer time at e'en;
And there as swift the waters pass
    So runs the life of man,
I sit me down upon the grass
    These beauties for to scan.

'Tis summer's day and dewy eve
    And sweet the sun sinks low,
I smile, and yet my heart will grieve
    To see the waters flow,
To see the flags that look so green,
    The sun gilt waves so bright.
I wander here this lovely e'en
    In wonder and delight.

The firs look dark on Clifford Hill,
    The river bright below,
All foamed beneath the water mill,
    While beauteous flowers do blow.
'Tis here I'd wander morn and night
    With fondly gazing eye,
To see the sunny golden light
    Go down in yonder sky.

Yes, dearly do these scenes I love,
    And dear that fir clad hill,
There all secure does build the dove,
    While click-clack goes the mill.
And now in Nature's sweet repose
    I leave this spot awhile;
The bee is buried in the rose,
    And man gone from his toil.

EVENING PRIMROSE

When once the sun sinks in the west,
And dew drops pearl the evening's breast,
Almost as pale as moonbeams are
Or its companionable star,
The evening primrose opes anew
Its delicate blossoms to the dew,
And shunning-hermit of the light,
Wastes its fair bloom upon the night,
Who blindfold to its fond caresses
Knows not the beauty it possesses.
Thus it blooms on till night is by
And day looks out with open eye;
'Bashed at the gaze it cannot shun,
It faints and withers and is done.

LABOUR'S LEISURE

O for the feelings and the careless health
That found me toiling in the fields — the joy
I felt at eve with not a wish for wealth,
When labour done and in the hedge put by
My delving spade — I homeward used to hie
With thoughts of books I often read by stealth
Beneath the blackthorn clumps at dinner's hour;
It urged my weary feet with eager speed
To hasten home where winter fires did shower
Scant light now felt as beautiful indeed,
Where bending o'er my knees I used to read
With earnest heed all books that had the power
To give me joy in most delicious ways,
And rest my spirits after weary days.

BIRDS

BIRDS' NESTS

How fresh the air, the birds how busy now,
In every walk if I but peep I find
Nests newly made or finished all and lined
With hair and thistledown, and in the bough
Of little hawthorn, huddled up in green,
The leaves still thickening as the spring gets age,
The pink's quite round and snug and closely laid,
And linnet's of materials loose and rough,
And still hedge sparrow, moping in the shade
Near the hedge bottom, weaves of homely stuff,
Dead grass and mosses green, an hermitage
For secrecy and shelter rightly made,
And beautiful it is to walk beside
The lanes and hedges where their homes abide.

THE REDCAP

The redcap is a painted bird
    And beautiful its feathers are,
In early spring its voice is heard
    While searching thistles brown and bare,
It makes a nest of mosses grey
    And lines it round with thistledown,
Five small pale-spotted eggs they lay
    In places never far from town.

I've seen them build on eldern boughs
    And tiptop of our russeting,
But never did I see till now
    A bird's nest in a garland hing,
In this old princifeather tree
    As hiding it from sudden showers,
The redcap's nest delighteth me
    Snug hid betwixt a bunch of flowers.

from *Birds Nesting*

BIRDS: WHY ARE YE SILENT

Why are ye silent?
Birds where do ye fly?
Winter's not violent
Wi' such a spring sky,
The wheatlands are green, snow and frost is away,
Birds why are ye silent on such a sweet day?

By the slated pig sty
The redbreast whispers,
Where brown leaves lie
The hedge sparrow lispers,
But why is the chaffinch and bullfinch so still,
While the sulphur primroses bedeck the wood hill?

The bright yellowhammers
Are strutting about,
All still and none stammers
A single note out,
From the hedge starts the blackbird at brookside to drink,
I thought he'd have whistled but he only said 'prink'.

The treecreeper hustles
Up fir's rusty bark,
All silent he bustles,
We needn't say hark,
There's no song in the forest in field or in wood,
Though the sun gilds the grass as though come in for good.

February the tenth and
Even sparrows scarce chirp,
The lark in the bents ran
And dodging round whirp,
All silent they winnow o'er grass i' the glen,
Then drop like a stone i' the stubbles agen.

How bright the odd daisies
Peep under the stubbs,
How bright pilewort blazes
Where riddled sheep rubs
The old willow trunk by the side o' the brook,
Where soon for blue violets the children will look.

By the cot green and mossy
Feed sparrows and hens,
On the ridge brown and glossy
They chirp now and then,
The wren cocks his tail o'er his back by the sty
Where his green bottle nest will be made by and by.

Here's bunches o' chickweed
Wi' small starry flowers,
Where redcaps oft pick seed
From weeds in spring hours,
And bluecap and blackcap in glossy spring coat
A-peeping in buds wi' out singing a note.

Why silent? should birds be,
And sunshine so warm,
Larks hide where the herds be
By cottage and farm,
If wild flowers were blooming and fully set in the spring,
Maybe all the birdies would cheerfully sing —

KINGFISHERS

Look there's two splendid feathered things
   Sit on that grey and stretching bough,
That from the leaning willow hings
   — Half o'er the gulling flood below;
Like foreign birds their feathers shine
   In splendour's rich and varied hue,
The peacock's tail is scarce as fine
   —Rich-shaded orange green and blue.

No finer birds are known to fly
   Than these gay dressed kingfishers are,
Who live on fish and watch the fry
   Of minnows nimbly passing there,
And there they'll sit whole hours away
   In that same lone and watching spot,
And when they dart to seize their prey
   Drop down as sudden as a shot.

Sandmartin-like they make a hole
   A steepy headlong bank beside,
As well as ever did the mole,
   And there their many eggs they hide,
And as is natural to their kind,
   Where mill dam waters wildly foam,
Places more hard to reach than find
   They choose, a safe and quiet home.

Their holes a full arm's length is made,
   Turned at the last with sudden bend,
Where lots of fishes' bones are laid
   Close to the large and farthest end;
Their eggs are white as wryneck's be
   And much about that middle size,
And boys oft skulk behind a tree
   To watch the old one where she flies,
And then pull out their knives in glee
   And delve in vain to reach the prize.

from *Birds Nesting*

57

THE CHIFFCHAFF

See at yon flitting bird that flies
    Above the oak tree tops at play,
Uttering its restless melodies
    Of 'chipichap' throughout the day;
Its nest is built on little bush
    Scarcely a foot above the ground,
Or hid in clumps of sedge or rush
    In woods where they are rarely found.

Its nest is like a oven made
    With moss and leaves and bits of grass,
And all so nice and snugly laid
    That hands may spoil but not replace;
It enters by a little hole,
    Its inside is a feather bed
From yards and poultry hovels stole,
    Its eggs are small and spotted red.

And all the spring and all the May,
    If I forbore the gate to clap,
Down that wood riding day by day
    I've heard it singing 'chipichap';
And o'er the tree tops seen it fly,
    Dancing about, a fairy thing,
But never yet could come so nigh
    To tell the colour of its wing.

from *Birds Nesting*

THE FIRST NIGHTINGALES

When first we hear the shy-come nightingales
They seem to mutter o'er their songs in fear,
And climbing e'er so soft the spinney rails
All stops as if no bird was anywhere.
The kindled bushes with the young leaves thin
Lets curious eyes to search a long way in,
Until impatience cannot see or hear
The hidden music — gets but little way
Upon the path — when up the songs begin
Full loud a moment and then low again.
But when a day or two confirms her stay,
Boldly she sings and loud for half the day,
And soon the village brings the woodman's tale,
Of having heard the new-come nightingale.

THE SKYLARK

The rolls and harrows lie at rest beside
The battered road, and spreading far and wide
Above the russet clods the corn is seen
Sprouting its spiry points of tender green,
Where squats the hare, to terrors wide awake,
Like some brown clod the harrows failed to break,
While 'neath the warm hedge boys stray far from home
To crop the early blossoms as they come
Where buttercups will make them eager run,
Opening their golden caskets to the sun,
To see who shall be first to pluck the prize;
And from their hurry up the skylark flies,
And o'er her half formed nest with happy wings
Winnows the air — till in the clouds she sings,
Then hangs a dust spot in the sunny skies,
And drops and drops till in her nest she lies
Where boys unheeding passed — ne'er dreaming then
That birds which flew so high — would drop agen
To nests upon the ground where anything
May come at to destroy. Had they the wing
Like such a bird, themselves would be too proud,
And build on nothing but a passing cloud,
As free from danger as the heavens are free
From pain and toil — there would they build and be
And sail about the world to scenes unheard
Of and unseen — O were they but a bird,
So think they while they listen to its song,
And smile and fancy and so pass along,
While its low nest moist with the dews of morn,
Lie safely with the leveret in the corn.

THE YELLOWHAMMER

When shall I see the whitethorn leaves agen,
And yellowhammers gathering the dry bents
By the dyke side on stilly moor or fen,
Feathered wi' love and nature's good intents?
Rude is the nest this architect invents,
Rural the place wi' cart ruts by dyke side,
Dead grass, horsehair and downy-headed bents
Tied to dead thistles she doth well provide,
Close to a hill o' ants where cowslips bloom
And shed o'er meadows far their sweet perfume.
In early spring when winds blow chilly cold
The yellowhammer trailing grass will come
To fix a place and choose an early home,
With yellow breast and head of solid gold.

LITTLE TROTTY WAGTAIL

Little trotty wagtail he went in the rain,
And tittering tottering sideways he ne'er got straight again,
He stooped to get a worm and looked up to catch a fly,
And then he flew away ere his feathers they were dry.

Little trotty wagtail he waddled in the mud,
And left his little footmarks trample where he would,
He waddled in the water pudge and waggle went his tail,
And chirrupt up his wings to dry upon the garden rail.

Little trotty wagtail you nimble all about,
And in the dimpling water pudge you waddle in and out,
Your home is nigh at hand and in the warm pigsty,
So little Master Wagtail I'll bid you a 'Goodbye'.

THE SWALLOW

Pretty swallow, once again
Come and pass me i' the rain,
Pretty swallow why so shy?
Pass again my window by...

Pretty little swallows fly
Village doors and windows by,
Whisking o'er the garden pales
Where the blackbird finds the snails...

On yon low thatched cottage stop,
In the sooty chimney pop,
Where thy wife and family
Every evening wait for thee —

QUAIL'S NEST

I wandered out one rainy day
    And heard a bird with merry joys
Cry 'wet my foot' for half the way;
    I stood and wondered at the noise,

When from my foot a bird did flee,
    The rain flew bouncing from her breast,
I wondered what the bird could be,
    And almost trampled on her nest.

The nest was full of eggs and round;
    I met a shepherd in the vales,
And stood to tell him what I found;
    He knew and said it was a quail's.

For he himself the nest had found
    Among the wheat and on the green,
When going on his daily round,
    With eggs as many as fifteen.

Among the stranger birds they feed,
    Their summer flight is short and slow,
There's very few know where they breed,
    And scarcely any where they go.

THE THRUSH'S NEST

Within a thick and spreading hawthorn bush
   That overhung a molehill large and round
I heard from morn to morn a merry thrush
   Sing hymns to sunrise, while I drank the sound
With joy, and often an intruding guest,
   I watched her secret toils from day to day,
How true she warped the moss to form her nest,
   And modelled it within with wood and clay,
And by and by like heath bells gilt with dew
   There lay her shining eggs as bright as flowers,
Ink-spotted over shells of greeny blue;
   And there I witnessed in the sunny hours
A brood of nature's minstrels chirp and fly,
Glad as that sunshine and the laughing sky.

THE RED ROBIN

Cock Robin he got a neat tippet at spring,
And he sat in a shed and heard other birds sing,
And he whistled a ballad as loud as he could,
And built him a nest of oak leaves by the wood,

And furnished it just as the celandine pressed
Like a bright burning blaze by the edge o' its nest,
All glittering with sunshine and beautiful rays,
Like high polished brass or the fire in a blaze.

Then sung a new song on the bend o' the brere,
And so it kept singing the whole of the year,
Till cowslips and wild roses blossomed and died,
The red robin sung by the old spring side.

SEDGE BIRD'S NEST

Fixed in a whitethorn bush, its summer guest,
    So low e'en grass o'er topped its tallest twig,
A sedge bird built its little benty nest
    Close by the meadow pool and wooden brig,
Where schoolboys every morn and eve did pass
    In robbing birds and cunning deeply skilled,
Searching each bush and taller clump of grass,
    Where'er was likelihood of bird to build;
Yet did she hide her habitation long
    And keep her little brood from danger's eye,
Hidden as secret as a cricket's song,
    Till they well-fledged o'er widest pools could fly,
    Proving that providence is often by,
To guard the simplest of her charge from wrong.

HEDGE SPARROW

The tame hedge sparrow in its russet dress
Is half a robin for its gentle ways,
And the bird-loving dame can do no less
Than throw it out a crumble on cold days.
In early March it into gardens strays,
And in the snug-clipped box tree green and round
It makes a nest of moss and hair, and lays
When e'en the snow is lurking on the ground
Its eggs, in number five of greenish blue,
Bright beautiful and glossy shining shells,
Much like the firetail's but of brighter hue.
Yet in her garden-home much danger dwells
Where skulking cat with mischief in its breast
Catches their young before they leave the nest.

THE FENS

AN EXTRACT

Among the tawny tasselled reed
The ducks and ducklings float and feed,
With head oft dabbling in the flood
They fish all day the weedy mud,
And tumbler-like are bobbing there,
Tails topsy-turvy in the air,
Then up and quack and down they go,
Heels over head again below.
The geese in troops come droving up,
Nibble the weeds and take a sup,
And closely puzzled to agree,
Chatter like gossips over tea.
The ganders with their scarlet nose,
When strife gets highest interpose,
And streeking necks to that and this,
With now a mutter now a hiss,
A nibble at the feathers too,
A sort of 'pray be quiet, do',
And turning as the matter mends,
He stills them into mutual friends;
Then in a sort of triumph sings
And throws the water o'er his wings...

ANIMALS AND INSECTS

BADGER

The badger grunting on his woodland track,
With shaggy hide and sharp nose scrowed with black,
Roots in the bushes and the woods and makes
A great huge burrow in the ferns and brakes,
With nose on ground he runs a awkward pace,
And anything will beat him in the race.
The shepherd's dog will run him to his den,
Followed and hooted by the dogs and men;
The woodman when the hunting comes about
Go round at night to stop the foxes out,
And hurrying through the bushes, ferns and brakes,
Nor sees the many holes the badger makes,
And often through the bushes to the chin
Breaks the old holes and tumbles headlong in.

When midnight comes a host of dogs and men
Go out and track the badger to his den,
And put a sack within the hole, and lie
Till the old grunting badger passes by;
He comes and hears, they let the strongest loose,
The old fox hears the noise and drops the goose,
The poacher shoots and hurries from the cry,
And the old hare half wounded buzzes by.
They get a forked stick to bear him down
And clapped the dogs and bore him to the town,
And bait him all the day with many dogs,
And laugh and shout and fright the scampering hogs.
He runs along and bites at all he meets,
They shout and hollo down the noisy streets.

He turns about to face the loud uproar
And drives the rebels to their very doors,
The frequent stone is hurled where'er they go,
When badgers fight and everyone's a foe.
The dogs are clapped and urged to join the fray,
The badger turns and drives them all away.
Though scarcely half as big, dimute and small,
He fights with dogs for hours and beats them all;
The heavy mastiff, savage in the fray,
Lies down and licks his feet and turns away,
The bulldog knows his match and waxes cold,
The badger grins and never leaves his hold.
He drives the crowd and follows at their heels
And bites them through — the drunkard swears and reels.

The frighted women takes the boys away,
The blackguard laughs and hurries in the fray,
He tries to reach the woods, a awkward race,
But sticks and cudgels quickly stop the chase.
He turns again and drives the noisy crowd
And beats the many dogs in noises loud,
He drives away and beats them every one
And then they loose them all and set them on.
He falls as dead and kicked by boys and men,
Then starts and grins and drives the crowd agen,
Till kicked and torn and beaten out he lies
And leaves his hold and cackles, groans and dies.

THE HEDGEHOG

The hedgehog hides beneath the rotten hedge
And makes a great round nest of grass and sedge,
Or in a bush or in a hollow tree;
And many often stoops and say they see
Him roll and fill his prickles full of crabs,
And creep away, and where the magpie dabs
His wing at muddy dyke in aged root
He makes a nest and fills it full of fruit,
On the hedge bottom hunts for crabs and sloes
And whistles like a cricket as he goes.
It rolls up like a ball, a shapeless hog
When gipsies hunt it with their noisy dogs;
I've seen it in their camps, they call it sweet,
Though black and bitter and unsavoury meat.

SQUIRREL'S NEST

One day when all the woods were bare and blea
I wandered out to take a pleasant walk
And saw a strange-formed nest on stoven tree
Where startled pigeon buzzed from bouncing hawk;
I wondered strangely what the nest could be
And thought besure it was some foreign bird,
So up I scrambled in the highest glee,
And my heart jumped at everything that stirred.
'Twas oval-shaped, strange wonder filled my breast;
I hoped to catch the old one on the nest
When something bolted out — I turned to see —
And a brown squirrel pattered up the tree.
'Twas lined with moss and leaves, compact and strong;
I sluthered down and wondering went along.

MOUSE'S NEST

I found a ball of grass among the hay
And progged it as I passed and went away,
And when I looked I fancied something stirred
And turned again and hoped to catch the bird,
When out an old mouse bolted in the wheat
With all her young ones hanging at her teats;
She looked so odd and so grotesque to me,
I ran and wondered what the thing could be,
And pushed the knapweed bunches where I stood;
When the mouse hurried from the crawling brood
The young ones squeaked, and when I went away
She found her nest again among the hay.
The water o'er the pebbles scarce could run,
And broad old cesspools glittered in the sun.

THE VIXEN

Among the taller wood with ivy hung
The old fox plays and dances round her young.
She snuffs and barks if any passes by
And swings her tail and turns prepared to fly,
The horseman hurries by, she bolts to see,
And turns again from danger never free.
If any stands she runs among the poles
And barks and snaps and drives them in the holes,
The shepherd sees them and the boy goes by
And gets a stick and progs the hole to try.
They get all still and lie in safety sure,
And out again when safety is secure,
And start and snap at blackbirds bouncing by
To fight and catch the great white butterfly.

THE WOOD IS SWEET

The wood is sweet, I love it well
    In spending there my leisure hours,
To look the snail its painted shell
    And search about for curious flowers,
Or 'neath the hazel's leafy thatch
    On a stulp or mossy ground,
Little squirrel's gambols watch,
    Oak trees dancing round and round...

                 from *Recollections after a Ramble*

HARES AT PLAY

The birds are gone to bed, the cows are still,
And sheep lie panting on each old molehill,
And underneath the willow's grey-green bough,
Like toil a-resting — lies the fallow plough.
The timid hares throw daylight's fears away
On the lane's road to dust and dance and play,
Then dabble in the grain by nought deterred
To lick the dew-fall from the barley's beard.
Then out they sturt again and round the hill
Like happy thoughts — dance — squat — and loiter still,
Till milking maidens in the early morn
Jingle their yokes and sturt them in the corn;
Through well-known beaten paths each nimbling hare
Sturts quick as fear — and seeks its hidden lair.

INSECTS

Thou tiny loiterer on the barley's beard,
And happy unit of a numerous herd
Of playfellows the laughing summer brings,
Mocking the sunshine in their glittering wings,
How merrily they creep and run and fly,
No kin they bear to labour's drudgery,
Smoothing the velvet of the pale hedge-rose;
And where they fly for dinner no one knows —
The dew drops feed them not — they love the shine
Of noon whose sun may bring them golden wine.
All day they're playing in their Sunday dress,
Till night goes sleep and they can do no less,
Then in the heath-bell's silken hood they fly,
And like to princes in their slumber lie,
From coming night and dropping dews and all,
In silken beds and roomy painted hall.
So happily they spend their summer day,
Now in the cornfields, now the new-mown hay,
One almost fancies that such happy things,
In coloured hoods and richly burnished wings,
Are fairy folk in splendid masquerade
Disguised, through fear of mortal folk afraid,
Keeping their merry pranks a mystery still,
Lest glaring day should do their secrets ill.

CLOCK–A–CLAY

In the cowslip's peeps I lie,
Hidden from the buzzing fly,
While green grass beneath me lies,
Pearled wi' dew like fishes' eyes.
Here I lie a clock-a-clay,
Waiting for the time o' day.

While grassy forests quake surprise,
And the wild wind sobs and sighs,
My gold home rocks as like to fall,
On its pillars green and tall;
When the pattering rain drives by
Clock-a-clay keeps warm and dry.

Day by day and night by night,
All the week I hide from sight,
In the cowslip's peeps I lie,
In rain and dew still warm and dry,
Day and night and night and day,
Red black-spotted clock-a-clay.

My home it shakes in wind and showers,
Pale green pillar topped wi' flowers,
Bending at the wild wind's breath,
Till I touch the grass beneath.
Here still I live, lone clock-a-clay,
Watching for the time of day.

THE LADYBIRD

Ladybird, Ladybird, where art thou gone?
Ere the daisy was open or the rose it was spread,
On the cabbage flower early thy scarlet wings shone,
I saw thee creep off to the tulip bed.
Ladybird, Ladybird, where art thou flown?
Thou wert here in the morning before the sun shone.

Just now up the bole o' the damson tree
You passed the gold lichen and got to the grey —
Ladybird, Ladybird, where can you be?
You climb up the tulips and then fly away.
You crept up the flowers while I plucked them just now
And crept to the top and then flew from the flowers.
O sleep not so high as the damson tree bough,
But come from the dew i' the eldern tree bowers.

Here's lavender trees that would hide a lone mouse
And lavender cotton wi' buttons o' gold,
And bushes o' lad's love as dry as a house,
Here's red pinks and daisies so sweet to behold.
Ladybird, Ladybird, come to thy nest,
The gold beds i' the rose o' the sweet brier tree,
Wi' rose-coloured curtains to pleasure thee best;
Come, Ladybird, back to thy garden and me.

THE ANTS

What wonder strikes the curious while he views
The black ants' city by a rotten tree
Or woodland bank — in ignorance we muse,
Pausing amazed, we know not what we see,
Such government and order there to be,
Some looking on and urging some to toil,
Dragging their loads of bent stalks slavishly,
And what's more wonderful — big loads that foil
One ant or two to carry, quickly then
A swarm flocks round to help their fellow men.
Surely they speak a language whisperingly,
Too fine for us to hear, and sure their ways
Prove they have kings and laws, and them to be
Deformed remnants of the fairy days.

SONGS

MEET ME IN THE GREEN GLEN

Love, meet me in the green glen
   Beside the tall elm tree,
Where the sweet-briar smells so sweet agen,
   There come wi' me,
      Meet me in the green glen.

Meet me at the sunset
   Down in the green glen,
Where we've often met
   By hawthorn tree and foxes' den,
      Meet me in the green glen.

Meet me by the sheep-pen
   Where briars smell at e'en,
Meet me i' the green glen
   Where whitethorn shades are green,
      Meet me in the green glen.

Meet me in the green glen
   By sweet-briar bushes there,
Meet me by your own sen
   Where the wild thyme blossoms fair,
      Meet me in the green glen.

Meet me by the sweet-briar
   By the molehill swelling there,
When the west glows like a fire
   God's crimson bed is there,
      Meet me by the green glen.

SONG

A SEABOY ON THE GIDDY MAST

A seaboy on the giddy mast
   Sees nought but ocean waves
And hears the wild inconstant blast
   Where loud the tempest raves.

My life is like the ocean wave
   And like the inconstant sea;
In every hope appears a grave,
   And leaves no hope for me.

My life is like the ocean's lot:
   Bright gleams the morning gave
But storms o'erwhelmed the sunny spot
   Deep in the ocean wave.

My life hath been the ocean storm,
   A black and troubled sea.
When shall I find my life a calm,
   A port and harbour free?

SONG

O WERT THOU IN THE STORM

O wert thou in the storm,
　　How I would shield thee,
To keep thee dry and warm,
　　A camp I would build thee.

Though the clouds pour'd again,
　　Not a drop should harm thee,
The music of wind and rain
　　Rather should charm thee.

O wert thou in the storm,
　　A shed I would build thee,
To keep thee dry and warm,
　　How I would shield thee.

The rain should not wet thee,
　　Nor thunderclap harm thee.
By thy side I would sit me,
　　To comfort and warm thee.

I would sit by thy side, love,
　　While the dread storm was over,
And the wings of an angel
　　My charmer would cover.

July 25th 1844

SONG

THE WIND WAVES O'ER THE MEADOWS GREEN

The wind waves o'er the meadows green
   And shakes my own wild flowers,
And shifts about the moving scene
   Like the life o' summer hours;
The little bents with reedy head,
   The scarce-seen shapes o' flowers,
All kink about like skeins o' thread
   In these wind-shaking hours.

All stir and strife and life and bustle
   In every thing around we see,
The rushes whistle, sedges rustle,
   The grass is buzzing round like bees.
The butterflies are tossed about
   Like skiffs upon a stormy sea,
The bees are lost amid the rout
   And drop in green perplexity.

Wilt thou be mine, thou bonny lass?
   Thy drapery floats so gracefully;
We'll walk along the meadow grass,
   We'll stand beneath the willow tree,
We'll mark the little reeling bee
   Along the grassy ocean rove,
Tossed like a little boat at sea,
   And interchange our vows of love.

SONG

I HID MY LOVE

I hid my love when young while I
Couldn't bear the buzzing of a fly,
I hid my love to my despite
Till I could not bear to look at light,
I dare not gaze upon her face
But left her memory in each place,
Where'er I saw a wild flower lie
I kissed and bade my love goodbye.

I met her in the greenest dells
Where dewdrops pearl the wood bluebells,
The lost breeze kissed her bright blue eye,
The bee kissed and went singing by,
A sunbeam found a passage there,
A gold chain round her neck so fair;
As secret as the wild bee's song
She lay there all the summer long.

I hid my love in field and town
Till e'en the breeze would knock me down;
The bees seemed singing ballads o'er,
The fly's buzz turned a lion's roar,
And even silence found a tongue
To haunt me all the summer long;
The riddle nature could not prove
Was nothing else but secret love.

SONG

ONE GLOOMY EVE I ROAMED ABOUT

One gloomy eve I roamed about
 'Neath Oxey's hazel bowers,
While timid hares were daring out
 To crop the dewy flowers,
And soothing was the scene to me,
 Right placid was my soul,
My breast was calm as summer's sea
 When waves forget to roll.

But short was even's placid smile
 My startled soul to charm,
When Nelly lightly skipped the stile
 Wi' milk pail on her arm.
One careless look on me she flung,
 As bright as parting day,
And like a hawk from covert sprung,
 It pounced my peace away.

Oxey Wood, a favourite spot of Clare's, is just
south of Helpston.

93

SONG

THE RAIN IS COME IN MISTY SHOWERS

The rain is come in misty showers,
    The landscape lies in shrouds,
Patches of sunshine like to flowers
    Fall down between the clouds
And gild the earth, elsewhere so cold,
With shreds like flowers of purest gold.

And now it sweeps along the hills
    Just like a falling cloud,
The cornfields into silence stills
    Where musty moisture shrouds,
And now a darker cloud sweeps o'er,
The rain drops faster than before.

The cattle graze along the ground,
    The lark she wets her wings
And chatters as she whirls around,
    Then to the wet corn sings,
And hides upon her twitchy nest,
Refreshed, with wet and speckled breast.

And I the calm delight embrace
    To walk along the fields
And feel the raindrops in my face
    That sweetest pleasure yields;
They come from heaven and there the Free
Sends down his blessings upon me.

I love to walk in summer showers
    When the rain falls gently down,
I love to walk a lecture hours
    A distance from the town,
To see the drops on bushes hing,
And blackbirds prune a dabbled wing.

EXPECTATION

A BALLAD

'Tis Saturday night and my shepherd will come
    With a hallo and whistle for me,
Be clear, O ye skies, take your storm-burthens home,
    Let no rain drench our favourite tree.
For I fear by the things that are hopping about
    There's a sign of a storm coming on,
The frog looks as black as the toad that creeps out
    From under its hiding stone.

The cat with her tail runneth round till she reels
    And the pigs race with mouthfuls of hay,
I sigh at the sight — and felt sick over meals,
    For I'm lone when my shepherd's away.
When dogs eat the grass it is sure to be rain,
    And our dog's in the orchard — e'en now
The swallows fly low and my heart is in pain,
    While the flies even maddened the cow.

The pigeons have moped on the cote the day long,
    And the hens went to bed before noon,
The blackbirds, long still, din the woods with their song,
    And they look upon showers as a boon,
While they keep their nest dry in the wet hazel bush,
    And moisten their black sooty wing,
Did they know but my sorrows they'd quickly be hush;
    Birds to make lovers happy should sing.

And I've often leaned o'er the croft's mossy gate
    To listen birds singing at night,
When I for the sure-footed Rover did wait,
    And rich was my bosom's delight.
And sweet had it been now I'm waiting anew
    Till the black snail is out from the grain,
But the south's ruddy clouds they have turned black
                      and blue,
    And the blackbirds are singing for rain.

The thrush 'wivy wit wivy wit' t'other night
    Sang aloud in the old sallow bush,
And I called him a pert little urchin outright
    To sing 'heavy wet' — and the thrush
Changed his note in a moment to 'cheer up' and 'cheer',
    And the clouds crept away from the sun,
Till my shepherd he came, and when thrushes I hear
    My heart with the music is won.

But the blackbird is rude and insulting, and now
    The more the clouds blacken the sky
The louder he sings from the green hazel bough,
    But he may be sad by and by,
For the cow-boy is stooping beneath the oak tree
    Whose branches hang down to the ground,
And beating his stick on the bushes to see
    If a bird startles out from the sound.

So silence is safety, and bird, have a care,
    Or your song will your dwelling betray,
For yesterday morning I saw your nest there,
    But sung not to fright ye away.
And now the boy's near you — well done, cunning bird,
    You have ceased and popped out t'other side,
Your nest it is safe, not a leaf has he stirred,
    And I have my shepherd descried.

THE MILKING MAID

How sweet the winds o' evening comes through the ash tree
boughs,
How sweet the milkmaid's soothing voice is calling up her
cows,
The bat is wheeling round the oak, the white moth round
the thorn,
And the lark is dropping to her nest i' the outside lands o'
corn.
The blue haze deepens wi' the green, the sun sets i' the gap,
The blue lift is the selfsame hue o' Bessey's bonny cap,
As she sits singing to herself upon her milking stool,
Beneath the oaks and willows by the old pond i' the cool.

O bonny is the milkmaid that sings beneath the shade,
O lovely is the wild rose cheek o' the bonny milking maid,
Her eyes turn on the cowslips so lovely to behold,
She thinks them like her earrings, rich pendant drops o'
gold.
The lilies o' the valleys — and you might fill a peck —
Is not so white as underneath her kerchief is her neck.
The daisies and the pileworts they make a garden show
Where the maiden sits a-milking by the thorn tree white as
snow.

What time beneath its crimson bank the orange setting sun
Sinks in the world o' spirits and leaves the earth i' dun,
The happy milking maiden wi' her well scoured milking pail
Goes tripping down the village street and singing down the
vale.
The pendant golden cowslips keep tapping at her gown,
She's minding where to set her feet and winna break them
down,
And I'll bestir myself and my hoe I'll strive to hide,
And gang to meet the milking maid down our burn side.

ON THE DEATH OF A SCOLD

A scolding woman's worse than hell,
    Her tongue can never cease,
She loves in quarrels to oppose,
    And hates the thoughts of peace.
So hags delight to see the storm
    Deform the smiling sky,
And joys to hear the thunder roll,
    And see the light'ning fly.
They know their tools is ready then
    To prosper every spell
Which the black arts of malice plans
    In journey work for hell,
But that which seems as choice in those
    Which bear the hellish mark
May be the effect of fear and dread —
    Hell's mysteries are dark.
'Tis said their bodies, when spells fail,
    Is like their souls condemn'd,
And when they fail of Nickey's prey
    He fox-like seizes them.
So of old scolding Nelly Trix
    The same thing may be said,
Who after marrying husbands six,
    And scolding all to dead,
She, looking out for further work,
    A seventh still desir'd,
But as experience makes fools wise
    Her customers grew tir'd,

So when her tongue could find no more
    To load with its abuse,
It silenc'd, not from being old
    But only want of use.
So Nickey, seeing trade had fail'd,
    And no one car'd to come,
He thought it time to shut up shop
    And instant took her home.

"written on an old woman with a terrible share of tongue who was actually married to a sixth husband and survived them" *(Clare's Autobiographical Writings)*

JOHN CLARE

MY EARLY HOME WAS THIS

Here sparrows built upon the trees
    And stock doves hide their nest,
The leaves were winnowed by the breeze
    Into a calmer rest,
The blackcap's song was very sweet
    That used the rose to kiss,
It made the paradise complete:
    My early home was this.

The redbreast from the sweet-briar bush
    Dropped down to pick the worm,
On the horse chestnut sang the thrush,
    O'er the home where I was born,
The dew morn like a shower of pearls
    Fell o'er this 'bower of bliss',
And on the bench sat boys and girls:
    My early home was this.

The old house stooped just like a cave
    Thatched o'er with mosses green,
Winter around the walls would rave,
    But all was calm within,
The trees they were as green agen
    Where bees the flowers would kiss,
But flowers and trees seemed sweeter then:
    My early home was this.

THY MERCY COVERS EARTH AND SKY

Thy mercy covers earth and sky,
    Thy love is everywhere,
Lord thou art rich, and so shall I
    If thou my wish wilt hear.

Lord let thy love and mercy grant
    Not what the rich pursue,
But just an honest start of want,
    And I am wealthy too.

Nor let my heart ungodly be
    To slight the little sent,
But feeling blessings come from thee
    Be happily content.

And if too covetous I grow
    Excuse a greedy prayer,
I crave what wealth can ne'er bestow,
    And thou alone canst spare.

I crave the guidance of thy will,
    The bliss of human kind,
A harmless heart afraid of ill,
    And a contented mind.

I LOVED THEE THOUGH I TOLD THEE NOT

I loved thee though I told thee not
    Right earlily and long,
Thou wert my joy in every spot,
    My theme in every song.

And when I saw a stranger face,
    Where beauty held the claim,
I gave it like a secret grace
    The being of thy name.

And all the charms of face or voice
    Which I in others see,
Are but the recollected choice
    Of what I felt for thee.

This poem seems addressed to Mary Joyce of
Glinton, Clare's first love and his poetic muse.

AFTER READING IN A LETTER PROPOSALS
FOR BUILDING A COTTAGE

Beside a runnel build my shed
    Wi' stubbles covered o'er,
Let broad oaks o'er its chimney spread
    And grass-plats grace the door.

The door may open wi' a string
    So that it closes tight,
And locks too would be wanted things
    To keep out thieves at night.

A little garden not too fine,
    Inclosed wi' painted pales,
And woodbines round the cot to twine,
    Pinned to the wall wi' nails.

Let hazels grow and spindling sedge,
    Bent bowering overhead,
Dig old man's beard from woodland hedge
    To twine a summer shade.

Beside the threshold sods provide
    And build a summer seat,
Plant sweet-briar bushes by its side
    And flowers that smelleth sweet.

I love the sparrows' ways to watch
    Upon the cotters' sheds,
So here and there pull out the thatch,
    As they may hide their heads.

And as the sweeping swallows stop
    Their flights along the green,
Leave holes within the chimney top
    To paste their nest between.

Stick shelves and cupboards round the hut
    In all the holes and nooks,
Nor in the corner fail to put
    A cupboard for the books.

Along the floor some sand I'll sift
    To make it fit to live in,
And then I'll thank ye for the gift,
    As something worth the giving.

'I AM'

I am — yet what I am, none cares or knows,
    My friends forsake me like a memory lost:
I am the self-consumer of my woes,
    They rise and vanish in oblivion's host
Like shadows in love's frenzied stifled throes,
And yet I am, and live — like vapours tossed

Into the nothingness of scorn and noise,
    Into the living sea of waking dreams
Where there is neither sense of life or joys
    But the vast shipwreck of my life's esteems;
Even the dearest, that I love the best,
Are strange — nay, rather stranger than the rest.

I long for scenes where man has never trod,
    A place where woman never smiled or wept,
There to abide with my Creator, God,
    And sleep as I in childhood sweetly slept,
Untroubling and untroubled where I lie,
The grass below — above the vaulted sky.

THE PEASANT POET

He loved the brook's soft sound,
    The swallow swimming by;
He loved the daisy-covered ground,
    The cloud-bedappled sky.
To him the dismal storm appeared
    The very voice of God,
And where the evening rock was reared
    Stood Moses with his rod.
And everything his eyes surveyed,
    The insects i' the brake,
Were creatures God almighty made;
    He loved them for his sake.
A silent man in life's affairs,
    A thinker from a boy,
A peasant in his daily cares —
    The poet in his joy.

GLOSSARY

agen, 1) against 2) again

baulk, narrow strip of grass between ploughed fields
bent, grass stalk
benty, made of dried grass stalks
besprent, besprinkle, moisten
bill, bill-hook
blackcap, great tit
blea, bleak, chilly
bluecap, blue tit
bottle, bundle of hay, straw or sticks
brere, briar
brig, bridge
brustling, bustling

cesspool, puddle on 'cess', i.e. land between a river and
         its bank when river is low
childern, children
clap, set dogs on
clock-a-clay, ladybird
corn bottle, cornflower
cote, dove-cot
cotter, cottager, farm tenant
crab, crab apple
crumping, crunching

dabbled, made wet or muddy
dead, death
dimute, diminutive
doubting, reluctant to depart
dropple, drop
droving, moving together

eldern, elder tree

firetail, redstart
flickering, quivering, fluttering
frit, frightened

gang, go
grains, main branches of trees
grass-plat, plot or patch of ground
gulling, washed out by water, hollowed

hing, hang
huswife, housewife

jobbling, stabbing
journey work, work done by a hired labourer

kid, bundle of firewood

lady-smock, cuckoo flower
landrail, corncrake
lecture hours, sermon time
lift, the sky, the heavens
lispers, lisps
lumping, threshing

nimble, nimbling, to dart, moving nimbly

old man's beard, traveller's joy

peep, single flower of a cluster, floret
pink, chaffinch
plat, plot
prick, prickle
princifeather, lilac (prince's feather)
prog, prod or poke
prune, preen (of bird's feathers)
pudge, small puddle

redcap, goldfinch
riddled, marked with ruddle, a red dye

rout, 1) route, way 2) bustle, commotion
russeting, russet apple

sawning, sauntering, loitering
scrowed, streaked
sedge bird, sedge warbler
sen, self
sluther, slither, slide
sprent, sprinkled
sputter, move fast causing commotion, splutter
stoven, tree stump
streeking, stretching
stubbs, stubble
stulp, tree stump
sturt, start, startle
suther, whistle, rush, sigh
sweeing, swaying, swooping
sweet-briar, wild rose with fragrant leaves

tarbottles, containing tar as a salve for sheep
tented, watched
throstle, song thrush
told, counted
touchwood, old decaying wood, readily inflammable
t'other, the other
twitchy, made of common couch grass

whirp, twist and turn
whitethorn, hawthorn
winna, will not
wi's with his
wont, as accustomed to be

younker, youngster

Index of first lines

117